Counselors in the Classroom
A Mainstream Psychoeducational Model for High-Risk Youth
Counselor-Teacher Guide

BETH WECHSLER, M.S.W.

Gosnold
Box CC Falmouth, MA 02540

Produced in association with
The Conservatory of American Letters
P. O. Box 298
Thomaston, Maine 04861

Library of Congress Catalog Card Number: 96-94070
ISBN# 0-89754-120-0

Introduction

At a time when drug use among teenagers is on the increase, educators and health care workers continue to search for new and innovative methods to combat the problem. The growing expectation that we have of our schools, to provide not only an education environment for our children, but also to assume more and more responsibility for social and human needs has created challenges and opportunities for all concerned about young people.

When Beth Wechsler first proposed the idea of "Counselors in the Classroom(CIC)", I was impressed by her vision to merge the clinical and academic entities into a model that could make a difference. The program was initiated in 1994 at a local regional high school and, soon after its introduction, began to demonstrate that it could produce meaningful change in the lives of young people at risk due to substance abuse. While the treatment programs at Gosnold have long provided assistance to the guidance counselors in local schools, CIC has generated an interest among school personnel that has been very encouraging. The model is effective because it is delivered in the "mainstream", not as an appendage to regular school activities. Integrating the service with classroom work promotes the involvement of faculty and without their support, positive results cannot be realized. The program has done that and more! We are now ready to move to the next phase of this development—training teachers and peers, eliminating the need for additional personnel to deliver the program and thus reducing overall costs.

The reception that CIC has received from school and human service workers is testimony to its unique and innovative approach. The program has been selected for presentation at major conferences in New England and at the Harvard Graduate School of Education. We believe that we have discovered something that has the potential to change the way human services are delivered in the school setting.

Beth Wechsler has realized her vision and achieved results well beyond her own expectations. We at Gosnold are please to have been part of the development of CIC and are confident that, as your school takes positive steps to address student drug abuse, you will find the program helpful.

Raymond V. Tamasi
President/CEO, Gosnold on Cape Cod

*"It's awfully hard to care about yourself
when you feel that no one cares about you"*

— 9th grade student

Counselors in the Classroom

A Mainstream Psychoeducational Model for High-Risk Youth

TABLE OF CONTENTS

I. Preface

We are in a time of major crisis in our junior and senior high schools.
The crisis stems from complex and confusing societal problems, but the root is clear:
the disintegration of large numbers of American families.

The students most visibly at risk appear to have two factors consistently in common. They are young people whose lives have been affected by drug or alcohol addiction in one or both of their parents and by divorce. These factors combined create an emotional environment that is both depriving and disorganizing. Inconsistent supervision and discipline, almost inevitably the outcome of parental addiction, and the stress attendant to the existence of addiction in a family, result in anxiety and depression, "cause difficulty in school, and other group settings, and result in deficient social and emotional coping skills"[1].

The children of these families comprise somewhere between twenty-five and fifty percent of our adolescent population. They arrive at school lacking internal ego functions that make learning, achievement, harmony, and mutual gain possible. Without comprehensive help of a specific nature these adolescents are at high risk for school failure. They stand at the gateway to adulthood positioned to take a path that will likely lead to more of the same problems from which they have come. Ahead of them is pregnancy too soon, single parenthood, lives likely to be undermined by alcohol and other drugs, job failure, welfare, mental and physical illness. From these parents to be, who are now adolescents, will come the next generation.

These students come through our junior and senior high schools at the end of childhood in the last phase of those years when change in the human personality can readily take place. They are young, hungry in many ways, starving for models of how to live, how to be in the world. Most are still open to attachment, but many do not have access to effective adults. It is only through attachment — relationships — that growth in personality which comes about through identification and internalization, can occur. The kind of relationships needed for this kind of learning, though they happen incidentally, are not the kind which schools at present either attempt or are structured to provide.

Curtis Collins, Massachusetts' Outstanding High School Principal and winner of the Bertram H. Holland award in 1995, is also a member of the Carnegie Commission For the Restructuring of the American High School for the 21st century. He remarks: "The repeated phrase that is heard at the Carnegie Commission meetings is that the roles of teachers must change".

If we are to rise to the challenges that face us as we approach the turn of the century, the roles of teachers and of school based counselors, until now largely separate in training and function, need to converge. The time has come for counselors to leave their offices and become part of the mainstream teaching team. We no longer have the luxury of a predominatly one to one setting. The need for our skills in developing the kind of relationships that facilitate emotional growth in students is now too broad and too great.

What follows is one response to the crisis in adolescent mental health. It is an approach that has been piloted using counselors in the classroom. It is not, as some might uneasily assume, that psychotherapy itself has come to school. Rather, we have attempted to offer a program within the mainstream curriculum that is designed to nourish through emotional attachment and structure (i.e. love and limits) school and peer bonding, and motivation for school and life success. Central to the course is both process and content. The course is geared toward improving ego function. The focus is on judgment, planning, and the ability to delay gratification — to look at the ramifications of actions, and to function for the good of the whole.

School-based prevention programs have predominately been directed to whole class or whole school populations. "Yet the intensity of the need is among the high-risk population"[2].

Specifically, this model identified a group of high-risk entering freshmen and attempted to provide, through the medium of a daily class and further individual contact as necessary, a stable, healthy extended family system at school.

For purposes of the pilot, we worked only with high-risk youth, utilizing existing part-time personnel, mainly restructuring rather than adding services. Within the financial realities that we face, both will ultimately be necessary. What we learned working with these students, how and why we eventually incorporated some of the central aspects of a twelve step program (with its documented power to facilitate change) is the story that follows.

It was our intent that the model we were developing might enable schools to begin to meet the emotional as well as educational needs of adolescents. By integrating services to high-risk youth into the curriculum itself, the design both mirrors the philosophy of the Massachusetts Education Reform Act and assists schools in complying with its student learning time regulations.

II. Adolescents in Crisis: Introduction

In the fall of 1993, I began to drive, two days a week, to a regional high school twenty-five miles from home. I had been hired by Gosnold, a drug and alcoholism treatment center, which had a contract to provide student assistance team services at Dennis Yarmouth Regional High School. It was the beginning of a historically tough Cape Cod winter, and it would precipitate in some form almost every one of the days that I drove to Yarmouth.

It was still September when Chris first stood in my doorway, a good looking 18 year old boy in jeans, a black leather jacket, and the mandatory gold earring. He sat in the armchair, at once filling the small office with the fresh scent of cigarettes, which were illegal on school grounds. "Are you the drug lady?" he wanted to know, "the one who knows how to get kids off pot?"

In the forty seven minutes that a high school period allows, Chris began to tell me his story. His parents were divorced, his father was an alcoholic. He had lived with his mother and her boyfriend until three years before when his mother had died. The boyfriend had promised to take care of Chris, but in a month's time he had found another woman. *Taking care of Chris* seemed to have come down to allowing him to continue to live in the apartment where Chris' SSI benefit had undoubtedly helped pay the rent.

Chris had been smoking pot daily and it was catching up with him. He had worked forty hours a week all summer, but smoked his paycheck. His girlfriend had left. He was a repeating senior on his way to nowhere. Now clean about a week, his grief and aloneness were starting to break through.

When the period was over, and another appointment made, he picked up his books and left the office. He was the first teenager I'd seen who had numbed his grief with marijuana. He would not be the last. I watched him go, still in his leather jacket which he had never removed. "This is an eighteen-year-old boy", I thought, "and he has no one".

In 1993 I had been a practicing M.S.W. for twenty-one years, all of them in children's services. I had worked with every kind of abuse, had seen dozens of "multiproblem" families, had represented children as Guardian Ad Litem in the courts, and had worked with the ones who had always held my heart, those in foster care. Chris was neither different nor more troubled than many of the children I had known.

What surprised me built slowly.

Week after week, I talked to adolescents in a clean, safe, well-run high school. The town had a reasonably mixed socioeconomic population. It was certainly no worse than, and in many ways much better than, most high schools across the country.

There were not enough hours in our two days a week contract for the students. It turned out their stories were grindingly the same. With the myriad variations possible in a human life of fourteen-plus years, the composite intake went like this. Susan or Melanie, Jared or Sean had parents who were divorced. One of their parents was an alcoholic or a drug addict, sometimes a year or two into recovery or, as often, still actively chemically dependent. One or both parents had remarried. Often they were still in conflict with each other over child support payments or visitation. Often, particularly if the student was acting out, he had bounced back and forth between his parents' homes. There were stepmothers or stepfathers or both (some of them sober, others not), stepbrothers and stepsisters. Parental time, money and affection were jealously fought over, heard in plaintive complaints about who had been given more clothes from The Gap, who had the larger bedroom, the new CD player. Often, the student lived with her mother. If that mother had not remarried, she had usually had boyfriends, at least some of whom had moved in and out. If one of the adults was chemically dependent, it was likely that somewhere along the line, someone had sexually abused the daughter.

"Melanie" sat in my office, her hair hanging over her face, her hands with their chewed fingernails, inked with a boyfriend's name. She had been detained and suspended for being late to class (or not getting there at all), for smoking in the bathroom or for being rude and disruptive. She usually avoided eye contact and her demeanor was surly. She was inclined to be defensive and rude when confronted by a teacher with anything less than tact. She did not have any idea how to stop making more trouble for herself nor was she sure that she wanted to. She was flunking, smoking pot, and drinking. If she had a boyfriend, she usually was obsessed with him. If he went out on her and made a move on another girl, the other girl was to blame.

Most of the time she would tell you everything if you would sit quietly and listen to her. Her story, like Jared's, Sean's and Christopher's, was the story of a family pie that had been cut into too many pieces. First, it had been sliced diagonally by paternal or maternal drug or alcohol addiction, then sliced again and again by divorce, remarriage, stepsiblings, then sometimes by another divorce.

The adolescents I met were starving to their emotional deaths. Though most had not been physically neglected, emotionally they were on their own and had been for a long time.

The thought that had first crossed my mind in September as Chris's black leather jacket receded from my view, would come back to me again and again. Here is another young person, only fourteen or fifteen years old, and (s)he doesn't have anyone.

There were so many of them.

Driven from the narrow scope of private practice by changes in third party payment, I had come back to the schools, where two decades before, I had begun my social work career. What I returned to was not what I had left.

I watched students passing in the hallways in the baggy prisoner style clothes that had become so appropriately the fashion, their lovely young bodies pierced with earrings in places that made me cringe — a walking visual testimony to their suffering and to their self images.

"What do you think about our kids?" the school's director of student services asked me one morning.

"I'm shell-shocked," I said. "I feel like I've been dropped into a war zone with a box of Band-Aids and a tube of Bacitracin".

I did what school counselors, social workers, and student assistance team personnel do all over the United States. I talked to students individually and in small groups. I called parents in, met with teachers, and referred some students to drug rehabilitation and others to AA. I referred students to outside agencies and private therapists. I assessed students who had been desperate enough to cut their arms or legs with razors to see whether they were suicidal. I talked to the Department of Social Services and to the court probation officers, occasionally wrote letters that infuriated parents, and met with the student's teachers. I referred students to the school's top quality Alternative Learning Program (ALP). They in turn referred their students to me. It was the bright spot in what otherwise seemed to be a bleak battleground.

The ALP model removes troubled students from the mainstream and provides them with an alternative classroom with enough personal contact, individualization and structure to enable many to succeed.

By January, it was obvious that the school needed to be able to accommodate three times as many students in the ALP setting. With the ALP and counseling, many students could get on their feet. Students at high-risk for school failure and dropping out need structure and individual support.

It existed and could be duplicated, but it wasn't going to be. As the crisis for American adolescents continued to climb, and national studies concluded that no less than 25% of high school students were at high-risk for school failure, school dollars for special services were waning. As test scores dropped, and the drop out and teen pregnancy rates climbed, the public was crying out for improved education and the model they had in mind was "Back To Basics". There would not be more money for services for high-risk students.

I learned three new concepts that year. The first of these had to do with *paradigms* (how one looked at a situation) and the importance, when you were stuck, of being able to make a "paradigm shift". The second was a message coming down to the schools from the Massachusetts Department of Education: *school restructuring*. The third was a repeated theme at this high school: *be proactive*.

I also learned something about the building in which I had landed. The principal, Curtis Collins, who the following year would be named High School Principal of the Year in Massachusetts, was disinclined to mediocrity and liked creativity. If a member of the faculty could come up with a design that seemed to make sense, (s)he was likely to get the go ahead to try it.

This was where things were; what there was to work with. I drove back and forth, through the snow laden winter of '94, trying to figure out what to do with little staff time, little money, and dozens of suffering, endangered and without intervention, potentially dangerous kids.

III. Adolescents in Crisis:
Review of the Literature

In 1991, The Harvard School Health Education Project released their study: "Creating An Agenda For School-Based Health Promotion: A Review of Selected Reports"[1] in draft form. What I will hereafter refer to as "The Harvard Report" reviews and synthesizes twenty four major studies and reports concerned with the health and educational status of children and youth in the United States. That study had in turn been modeled on a review of 22 reports (1983-1988) "Social Policy for Children and Families: Creating An Agenda"[2]. The literature confirmed that what we were observing in microcosm in local high schools was indeed a national crisis. Even the percentages looked the same.

The Code Blue Report notes: "For the first time in the history of this country, young people are less healthy and less prepared to take their places in society than were their parents"[3].

A 1990 report of the American Medical Association (America's Adolescents: How Healthy Are They?) identified the major health threats not as biomedical, but as a result of social environment and behaviors that is largely preventable — "social morbidities": suicide, homicide, substance abuse, pregnancy, sexually transmitted diseases, HIV. The largest number of adolescents considered at risk for death and poor health are so as a result of social environment and behaviors [4].

The same statistics have emerged repeatedly. The AMA study suggested that 25% of adolescents lead high-risk lifestyles. Joy Dryfoos' 1990 book *Adolescents at Risk*, which also summarized multiple studies, concluded that 25% of ten to seventeen-year-olds were at high risk for encountering serious problems and suggested that an additional 25% were at "moderate high-risk"[5]. The Carnegie Counsel on Adolescent Development, Task Force on Education of Young Adolescents also found one fourth of adolescents age ten to seventeen "vulnerable to multiple high-risk behaviors"[6].

Approximately one child in four is at risk because of substance abuse, early unprotected intercourse, delinquency, and school failure.

Deborah Prothrow-Stith, M.D., assistant dean for government and community programs at the Harvard School of Public Health describes the growing epidemic of youth violence. Frances Stott, Ph.D., dean of academic programs at the Erikson Institute for Advance Study in Child Development, attributes the rise to the increase in single parent families, divorce, substance abuse and domestic violence which places enormous pressure on both adults and children.

There are seven million young people in the United States in dire need of intensive care. Another seven million are involved in some level of behavior that poses a significant threat to their health and to the quality of their lives. From these data, the reports drew similar conclusions:

1. Misapplication of national resources and disruption of parenting have resulted in child neglect on a massive scale[7].

2. Without appropriate programs "large number of adolescents will fail educationally, fail as effective parents and fail as productive members of the economy...we must act immediately"[7].

3. Education and health are interrelated. Education impacts health and conversely health affects education. "Efforts to improve school performance that ignore health are ill-conceived." "Increasing academic achievement will require attending to health in the broadest sense"[8].

4. "Health promotion and education efforts should be centered in and around schools." (Harvard Report, p.3)[9].

The National Association of the State Boards of Education (NASBE) recommended that each school make adolescent health a priority. To do so, the NASBE advised that schools:

- Become a far more personal institution that treats adolescents as individuals, increasing their affiliation with the school;

- Become a far more positive learning environment that engages adolescents' interest and motivates them to want to achieve their potential;

- Provide students with a new kind of health education;

- Improve collaboration inside and outside of schools to assure that students receive help with physical, social and emotional problems that are interfering with their learning.

At a time when the behaviors that we label "high-risk" are receiving increasing attention in our schools, what then is the "state of the art"?

In every guidance office a stack of catalogues offers computer software, videos, visual aids, books, magazines, games, curriculum guides, posters and tee-shirts. Materials are available that tell a child everything he might ever want to know (and far more than any sensible parent would wish) about alcohol, cocaine, marijuana and steroids. There are portable drug identification kits ($219.95), "Smokey Sue" in a durable carrying case, a "smoked lung" made of BIOLITE. There are videos to enhance self esteem, handle emotions, and deal with pressure. There are coloring books to teach elementary school kids "How To Say No". Complete educational video packages teach anger control and communication, or take the health teacher off the hot seat of sex education. There are gang intervention handbooks and a seemingly infinite selection of pamphlets for everything from addiction to youth power.

The state of the art of intervening with high-risk behaviors is reflected in the myriad of materials offered. Though research makes clear that single prong efforts offer little long term value, we continue to struggle with delinquency, substance abuse, teen pregnancy and school failure as if they were unrelated events, and more significantly, as if they were problems that might be solved by the creative transmission of information. Categorical materials exist in dazzling profusion. Teenagers know all the jargon. They know what codependency is, that alcoholism is progressive, and how many drinks it takes to flunk a breathalyzer test.

We have infinite software for a computer system that no one is quite certain how to operate. What is lacking is an overall structure in which learning, of the kind that leads to changes in thinking and ultimately in behavior, is likely to occur.

Many of the problem behaviors that we call h..gh-risk are interrelated. It is the teenage girl who drinks who is at the highest risk for rape, battering, pregnancy, and sexually transmitted disease. It is the same girl whose parents are more than likely divorced and addicted who is likely to have been abused and probably is still being neglected. The same student is frequently absent and doing poorly in school. In fact, "Low achievement in school has been shown to be an important predictor of substance abuse, delinquency, and early sexual intercourse"[10] (Dryfoos p .79).

Dryfoos identified six characteristics as predictive of high-risk behaviors. These were early occurrence of the problem behavior, poor school performance, behavior problems, low resistance to negative peer influence, insufficient parental bonding and guidance, and poverty.

Dryfoos states: "In many diverse ways, delinquency, early initiation of smoking and alcohol use, heavy drug use, unprotected sexual intercourse, early childbearing and school failure and dropping out are interrelated. Every young person who has sex at 12 does not become a drug addict or a felon, but most drug addicts experienced early sexual encounters and some form of delinquent behavior. The goal of interventions is to assist children to pursue a life path that leads to responsible adulthood."

If there is a single, overpowering conclusion that the literature draws, it is that fragmentation of programs and services is one of the main barriers to effective intervention. Health and education systems often work without any real collaboration. Elisabeth B. Schorr and Daniel Schorr sum it up:

> "Whether it be medical care, social services or education, when those in greatest need do receive services, they are likely to be too fragmented and too meager to accomplish their purpose...What it comes down to is that, for the children of the shadows, rotten outcomes— even risk factors—cannot be prevented by simplistic one-pronged approaches anymore... Many interventions have turned out to be ineffective not because seriously disadvantaged families are beyond help, but because we have tried to attack complex, deeply rooted tangles of troubles with isolated fragments of help"[11].

Dryfoos agrees: "...why is the status of high-risk youth deteriorating?...Success is elusive because the programs as interventions are too fragmented and weak to have enough impact. They do not create change..."

We have sufficient research. Successful methods have been identified. Change is created by programs that do more than provide information. Successful programs for high-risk youth:

- help to develop their skills in coping, stress management and decision making
- are comprehensive, intensive, and family and community oriented
- utilize staff with time and skills to develop relationships of respect and collaboration
- provide individual attention, attaching high-risk youth to a responsible adult who pays attention to that child's specific needs
- focus on early identification and intervention
- seek to involve parents
- focus in schools
- are often administered by agencies outside of schools
- link to the world of work.

Specific to substance abuse intervention, Dryfoos identifies three types of programs as the most successful: *school-based social skills curricula, school-based counseling services,* and *multicomponent collaborative community programs.* In her keynote address at the 1995 Hartman Conference on Children and Families, Dryfoos further identified the need at the high school level "to find someone — an advocate — to whom the adolescent can be attached" as opposed to striving for parental involvement "because it is so difficult to maintain parental involvement at the high school level".

IV. A Mainstream Model for Intervention
With High-risk Youth

"Counselors in the Classroom" was designed to incorporate the major conclusions of the adolescent health research. We would add a comprehensive, intensive component to our traditionalal student assistance model. We set out to develop a program that would be:

- intensive
- staffed by personnel with time and skills to develop relationships of collaboration and respect
- able to attach high-risk students to a responsible adult who would pay attention to that student's needs
- located in the school
- administered by an agency outside the school
- committed to parent involvement, and
- focused on social skills training.

The reputation of the 8th grade classes in the Dennis and Yarmouth middle schools preceded them by a year to the high school. The towns' police liaison officers, who served both the middle and high school buildings, were spending the majority of their time at the middle schools. Substance abuse was beginning earlier and manifesting itself more broadly, behavior problems proliferated, including instances of harassment. Virtually unheard of on Cape Cod, there was a gang.

We decided to target the entering freshmen. If we met with students daily in the classroom for "structured learning time", they could receive elective credit for their time with us. This constituted a radical restructuring in the delivery of mental health services. By devising an elective course for the students we sought to serve, counseling would become part of the curriculum rather than an ancillary "support" service. This would make it possible to dramatically increase the amount of time the students would have with us and with each other.

Targeted freshmen would be young people currently, or at risk of becoming, drug or alcohol abusers. Selected students would have experienced (no less than two, and most often three or more) of the following criteria:

- repeated school failure
- high absence rate
- history of substance abuse
- child of a substance abuser
- history of being abused
- mental health problems
- living with other than two natural parents
- attempted suicide
- attention deficit disorder.

At the time that the freshman course which we called "LifeSkills", was conceived, the administration anticipated funding an increase from twelve to thirty hours weekly of Gosnold staff time. Then, funding was cut back. The pilot would have died during gestation, but for a call from a counseling student in a local master's program. She was seeking a site and a supervisor. Student Assistance Team services, comprised now of one twelve hour/week clinician and a twenty hour/week intern, would go into the classroom in September, 1994.

The class would meet daily first semester, perhaps three days/week the second semester. We intended to maintain contact with our students from the time they arrived at high school until the day they left.

I worked on the curriculum in the spring. In line with the literature, and fundamental to all counseling training, freshman "LifeSkills" would focus first and foremost on attachment and connection. We would try to form relationships with the students and to help them form positive relationships with one another. We would endeavor to help them "affiliate" with Dennis-Yarmouth Regional High School. Hirschi's control theory 1 (1969) suggests that delinquency and other forms of negative behavior are produced by weak commitment to family, schools, positive peers and to the community. Strong, positive bonding to people and institutions leading to more positive behavior would coincide with attachments, involvement in positive activities and a belief in the importance of the general well-being of all.

The center of our plan was to create a classroom environment and sufficient relationship with both peers and adults so that modeling and learning of the types that lead to the development of personal and social competence could occur. We believed this would be intrinsic to motivating students for school success.

We would access the large existing body of educational materials designed to teach organization and planning, goal setting, decision making, and critical thinking skills. Whenever possible, we would focus on drug and alcohol awareness, emphasizing the issues that arise for children of alcoholics.

We found that our goals echoed those in The Massachusetts Common Core of Learning —

> **To help students learn to STUDY AND WORK EFFECTIVELY:**
> *Set goals and achieve them by organizing time, work space, and resources effectively.*
> *Monitor progress and learn from both successes and mistakes.*
> *Manage money, balance competing priorities and interests, and allocate time among study,*
>   *work and recreation.*
> *Work both independently and in groups.*
> *Work hard, persevere and act with integrity.*
>
> **To help students learn to DEMONSTRATE PERSONAL, SOCIAL AND CIVIC RESPONSIBILITY:**
> *Accept responsibility for one's own behavior and actions.*
> *Treat others with respect and understand the differences among people.*
> *Learn to resolve disagreements, reduce conflict and prevent violence.*
> *Participate in meaningful community and/or school activities.*

These were the long term goals.

Initially, we hoped simply to engage the students with "LifeSkills" counselors and with each other. Since the course was new, it was likely to "live or die" based on the reputation it established with students.

We hoped the first semester would enable students to see "LifeSkills" as a good place to be and school success as possible for themselves. To do this, we would have to create a structure that would support behaviors appropriate to the high school setting and to school success.

V. The First Semester

We began with seven 14-year-olds: four girls and three boys, all already failing coming out of 8th grade. One of the girls, whose prior school history had been more favorable, had been in treatment and seemed to be back on her feet. After meeting with her mother, we agreed that she had not been correctly placed and she was transferred out of "LifeSkills".

Of the remaining six, two had fathers whose whereabouts were long unknown. A third father was in prison. Of the remaining nine biological parents, seven were believed to be active addicts or alcoholics; one was in recovery. Three students had mothers who were essentially out of the picture. The six students had only two, present, sober, biological parents among them. Two students lived with their grandfathers. None lived in an intact family, nor in an entirely sober one.

Two of the girls had been sexually abused, and we had questions about another. Four had substance abuse histories. We believed that the remaining two used. We believed two of the girls had been promiscuous.

The counseling intern was Barbara Crellin, a second-year student in the Lesley College Masters in Education Program. A former teacher, her background, maturity and general good sense allowed her a much higher skill level than would ordinarily be found in an intern. We greeted the students together the first two days of class. Once underway, Barbara would meet with them three days a week. I would meet them once. We would see them together on the fifth day. Although not ideal, it was all that was possible. Barbara and I talked by phone almost daily to bridge the gap.

Also far less than ideal, we were not able to do preliminary interviews with our students. We had selected students based on recommendations made by middle school faculty. Invitations to participate in the class had been made by telephone calls to parents. The students were prepared for the class only indirectly. None had met with us.

When the students realized what "LifeSkills" was about, which took less than a single period, they were horrified. No matter how enthusiastically we presented the class to them, they had clearly been singled out. The small class size increased their discomfort. They felt stigmatized at the beginning of their high school careers. It flew in the face of their largely unarticulated fantasies that, without actually having to do anything to create change, everything would go well for them now that they were in high school.

The curriculum did not interest them. "NameNiks" (name tags with attributes) were more than they could handle. We could not motivate them to suggest prospective class trips that we intended them to be able to earn. They did not want to go anywhere with us or one another. They looked around and decided: the others were "losers".

They had our number. We were counselors. They didn't need counselors, or "LifeSkills". Maybe the other students in the room did, but nothing was the matter with them.

Within forty-eight hours, all six students approached their guidance counselor separately to request transfer out of the class. It was not an auspicious beginning.

It was decided that students would not be allowed to drop without a parent conference. One parent came to school; she decided that her daughter should stay the semester.

They were stuck with us.

The adolescent repertoire of behavior that communicates "I don't want to be here" is fairly limited. Over a two-decade career, I had talked into flat eyes and expressionless faces, worked to coax even the beginning of a smile from compressed lips as I faced arms folded across chests. Now there were six of them able to play off one another for the forty-seven minutes that faced either the intern or me at the end of every school day.

They straggled into the classroom slumped over, dropping their backpacks with a thud. We greeted each of them directly, with little reply. Later, after attending a conference with Claire LaMeres, we began to shake hands with them. Once seated, they sighed, yawned and stared out the window, pulled their hats over their eyes, rolled pencils across their desktops, talked to each other, hooted, and pleaded to go the bathroom. For the most part, they were not truly rude, nor were they aggressive. We were careful not to embarass or belittle them.

Whatever we offered them was "boring". They questioned our selection of activities, wondering whether they came from a 7th grade workbook. They dissolved during role plays, complained about the videos and became agitated whenever we tried to talk about alcohol and drug use. More than once, until we called a parent and suggested a urine screen, we suspected that some were stoned.

The best-dressed of the girls refused to participate at all, conveying unrelentingly to us, but more importantly to the group, that she felt herself superior. If the boys' behavior was more uneven and they required the majority of our prompts, they also gave us more. Occasionally, the boys had "good days". In general, in these always co-ed classes, they talked more and engaged more readily.

By and large, the group was for us (and for their other teachers) unteachable.

We struggled with some critical issues in our role. Like Sagittarius, we were half one thing, half something else. As counselors, we listened empathically and focused on feelings. As teachers, we needed to keep students on track, and had to set limits. The agitation and unhappiness of the students, their distrustfulness and unspoken agendas, challenged us daily.

Off what was for us "center stage", there was much more going on in our students' lives. We followed their crises and saw the desperation of their realities. We made a decision to make individual counseling available to them; formal weekly sessions with the intern for those who wanted them, an open door policy overall. The decision to see students individually was and continues to be open to debate. Our group therapy consultant advised against it. If students talked to us individually, they would be less likely to talk in the group.

We tried a range of curricula during the first semester. It was difficult to keep the students on track. We worked to establish relationships with students, toward group trust, and group norms that supported school success.

Some of what we implemented during the first term, we stayed committed to as central to the program design.

1. We distributed student planners and checked them daily.

High-risk students exhibit many of the traits found in students with Attention Deficit Disorder Hyperactivity Disorder (ADHD). ADHD students lose things necessary for tasks. According to the Massachusetts Department of Education article "A Focus on Attention Deficits ", "Adolescents with attention deficits often appear to be turned off by academic tasks. They tend to be poor listeners, notetakers and copiers...disorganization is prominent; students have difficulty writing down and remembering assignments, and difficulty budgeting time"[1].

Mary Jane Beach, LCSW, co-director of Bridges, a counseling practice specializing in students with learning disabilities and more recently in treatment of ADHD, says "To build the structure with these students is 90% of the gain. Structuring comes prior to psychotherapy or medication. Schedules and routines, assignment books and planners are central. ADHD is a breakdown in the executive functions of the brain, so you help ADHD students with planning and timekeeping".

Planners were our main pilot expenditure that fall, totaling less than $70.00. We used a commercial student planner. Second semester we shifted to one that also contained an address book.

If the planners were checked daily, students brought them. When we attempted to shift to intermittent reinforcement two months into the school year, letting a day or two lapse between planner checks, we found they were not ready. High-risk students require clear expectations and a level of structure that would normally be necessary for a much younger child. Expecting them to manage with less direction sets them up for more failure.

For some of these students it may indeed be attention deficit disorder, a neurological breakdown in the executive function of the brain. But for many of our students, the disorganized, anxiety-producing environment of the alcoholic family system may explain the behaviors. Simply put, most high-risk students have never lived in an environment that helped them organize themselves. Which comes first: addiction or attention deficit?

2. We made ourselves available to the students.

Group process came first. We intended to convey to students that what they felt they needed was, if only in this classroom, as important to us as the content of the work. If they would use the group to talk about their difficulties, i.e. if they could do so "productively", we would temporarily put aside whatever curriculum we had planned. This strategy provided opportunities for the best kind of teaching, "on the fly". We could role play an alternative to an aggressive confrontation. We tried to help them confront one another appropriately. When both the intern and I were in the room together, we could model an adult partnership that many of them had never observed. The potential of the model was infinite and on the occasional "good days" we felt the value of what we were trying to do.

During the other six periods of the day, whenever our schedules allowed, we kept our door open. They began to drop in on us, to complain about a perceived injustice, a scrape they had gotten into, to ask for a piece of candy from the jar on Barbara's desk. After awhile, some simply came, like young children to their mothers, to reconnect, to be reassured by her presence. Barbara was at the high school four days a week. The students, especially those she saw both in the classroom and individually, quickly became attached to her.

As we had intended, the students came to us, too, with serious problems: a parental diagnosis of cancer, an incident of physical abuse that led to temporary foster care, a breaking and entering that a student allowed us to guide him into confessing to the police.

3. We fed them.

The plan had been to implement a comprehensive behavior modification system. Initially, we allowed student resistance to derail us. Eventually, we instituted the system one component at a time.

If all arrived on time for class every day, then on Friday we provided a snack. Our high-risk freshmen turned out to be an avid "milk and cookies" crowd. They entertained us with discussions of whether they wanted brownies or chocolate chip cookies. As intended, they brought pressure to bear on stragglers, whose between periods excursions to the bathroom for a cigarette jeopardized their Friday treat. In January we started giving cookies to any student who arrived with an A, B, or C paper from another class.

Occasionally, we took them out of the building. Just before Christmas they chose to visit a nursing home where they surprised us by how appropriately and kindly they behaved with Alzheimer's patients. "Are we going soon?" whispered one of the most recalcitrant of the 9th grade boys. He had taken me tactfully aside an hour into the visit. "This is really hard." They were far less kind at lunch when a waiter with effeminate mannerisms served our table. The boys could not handle themselves and it generated a conversation about tolerance.

But by and large, though we continued to feel that the model was right, our successes felt limited. We had more "bad" days than "good" ones with the class. Time with the students was far less productive than we had projected. Suspensions and absences were frequent. "F" in other classes was a common grade.

When we left on Christmas break, most of the students still conveyed their intention to leave the class at the end of the semester. We could not honestly tell ourselves that we hated to see them go.

VI. The Steps to School Success

A. *Incorporating the Principles of Alcoholics Anonymous*

We were stuck. The group, though they would have denied that they were one, consistently over-powered our efforts to progress. Both individually and in unison, their approach was "not to feel and not to deal". We were strangling on the same dynamic that family members experience when living with an addict. Neither truth nor the greater good had relevancy. Something in the internal processes of the individuals barred our way.

We wondered whether we had a class of fourteen-year-old addicts. Both individually and in the classroom, all professed to former alcohol and drug use. All denied present use. Two drug screens that we asked parents to obtain came back negative. We would have bet otherwise, but negative they were.

All of the students were children of alcoholics (COAs). They relied on the psychological defenses that addicts use. It was what they had experienced and observed, the model of thought and action that had been taught to them. Whether or not they were actively using chemicals, the students thought and acted like active alcoholics and addicts.

They had shortfalls in the executive functions of the ego that monitor reality testing, reasoning, judgment and planning. They had difficulty perceiving the consequences of their behavior, delaying gratification and profiting from their mistakes. They relied predominantly on the entrenched psycho-logical defenses typically found in alcoholic family systems: denial, avoidance and projection. These defenses consistently blocked the development of a stronger ego.

All were also traumatized children and the same dynamics can be explained from the perspective of trauma, leading in turn to anger, depression and increased risk of substance abuse.

Craig Nakken, in *The Addictive Personality*, describes the true start of an addictive relationship as occurring when a person "repeatedly seeks the illusion of relief to avoid unpleasant feelings or situations". He calls this "nurturing through avoidance", the search for serenity "through an object or event". The feeling of discomfort becomes for the addict a signal to act out, to strive to alleviate pain, not by dealing with its source but by the use of something. Nakken writes, "Every time addicts choose to act out in an addictive way, they are saying to themselves one or more of the following:

> I don't really need people.
> I don't have to face anything I don't want to.
> I'm afraid to face life's and my problems.
> Objects and events are more important than people.
> I can do anything I want, whenever I want, no matter whom it hurts"[1].

"Addiction starts to create the very thing the person is trying to avoid — pain. The addict seeks refuge from the pain of addiction by moving further into the addictive process."

This was our small group of ninth-graders. Fear, overwhelming hurt and the failure of the environment to nurture the development of a strong ego had left them with neither the hope nor the drive to build a decent, fulfilling life for themselves. What they had already experienced of life did not inspire them to try to live fully. Their experience of their lives as hopeless undermined their willingness to strive. If they were not already addicts, they were psychologically addicts, addicts in the making. We had nothing in our arsenal strong enough to disrupt the progression. Our curriculum did not accurately target what AA members aptly call "Stinking Thinking".

I took the twenty third printing of "Twelve Steps and Twelve Traditions"[2] with me to Florida over Christmas. When our plane was delayed going home, I first drafted (in the airport waiting area) an adaptation of the 12 Suggested Steps of AA. We began to hold "Step Meetings" in January 1995, always accompanied by a cup of hot chocolate. We had three weeks left in the semester.

B. Alcoholics Anonymous

Alcoholics Anonymous (AA) began in Akron, Ohio in 1935. Two professionally successful men, both severe alcoholics, co-founded the AA fellowship. The basic principles that formed the cornerstone of their recovery were taken from the fields of both religion and medicine.

"Alcoholics Anonymous" was published in 1939 and the rest, of course, is history. Today Alcoholics Anonymous numbers well over a million success stories, and meetings can be found all over the globe. The program, based on the "Twelve Steps and Twelve Traditions", has been used to facilitate recovery from addictive behaviors that include drug abuse, eating, gambling, smoking, child abuse, co-dependency, and sexual addiction.

To my knowledge, AA had never before been adapted for public school use. The reason for that seemed obvious: AA is a spiritual program, centered on the concept of a "higher power" (however one chooses to perceive that power) and therefore rightly "inadmissible" in an American public school. On the other hand, the basic concept of breaking knowledge down into "steps", guiding principles, predates AA and even Christianity: Buddhism.

Twelve Steps, as a colleague in recovery remarked, is too many for most of us. Our fourteen-year-old students could not do twelve. I settled for Five Steps, which follow closely the formula used in the first steps in AA, and omitted any reference to a "higher power".

Step One: *We admitted that we were failing school, that the way in which we were thinking and living would not allow us to succeed.*

Step Two: *We made a commitment. We would follow, as exactly as we were able, the program for school success that was being offered to us.*

Step Three: *We understood and accepted the need for abstinence from alcohol and all other drugs.*

Step Four: *We got honest with ourselves.*

Step Five: *We would bring something of ourselves, beyond our schoolwork, to school. We would identify what that was by listening to our own hearts.*

C. The A.A. Method in the Classroom

The Alcoholics Anonymous structure (on which Step By Step To School Success is based) uses the following features in program delivery. The "Twelve Steps and Twelve Traditions" is written in the first person plural ("we") and the voice itself conveys universality, an "I'm not talking down to you" and "we're all in this together" tone along with "here's the path". This has been adopted in the School Success Steps.

Step meetings in the anonymous programs rotate the person who chairs the meeting, so that each participant has a chance to assume the leadership role and also to "qualify" himself. In these programs, qualifying means explaining why one has the right to be speaking about the problem. By definition, all of our "LifeSkills" students are qualified to speak about school failure.

At step meetings, the group is seated in a circle. The steps are read at the rate of one each week. After the fifth week, the group returns to step one and begins to read the steps again. Thus, the group goes over each step once every five weeks. On the other days, the class continues to focus on other aspects of the curriculum.

Central to the AA structure is the concept of sponsorship. Newcomers in recovery programs are encouraged to make a connection to someone who has a trustworthy period of recovery. In AA this is two years of sobriety. In a new program there are, by definition, few available sponsors. Certainly, there is no one who has two years of "recovery" (in this case, school success) "in the program".

For adolescents, peer sponsors are even more important. We located one student in the ALP who was making a good recovery both from drug abuse and school failure. She had been actively involved in A.A. and N.A. and was familiar with the approach and enthusiastic about the adaptation to the school. She agreed to join the class for their weekly step meetings.

Such a student can be a critical factor in the group's dynamics. He or she must be selected with enormous care since (s)he is being set up as a role model. Once selected, the older student needs and deserves careful support from faculty both in the classroom and between step meetings. It is critical to have enough relationship with the sponsor that if he has a slip, he is able to tell you. Otherwise, the dishonesty has enormous negative consequences and can potentially undermine not only the sponsoring student but the entire group. Even a slip can be utilized positively and framed, in A.A. language, as a "convincer".

The students in the program themselves show great motivation to become sponsors. We would consider two semesters with a solid "C" average and without significant disciplinary incident or absenteeism to constitute the minimum qualification for sponsoring. The potential exits to foster a school-based "sponsoring system". Students who have been failing in school and are now experiencing success could bring (in A.A. language) "their experience, strength, and hope" to their peers.

Another central aspect of the Anonymous programs is the concept of "taking inventory." This is a method that helps addicts look honestly at themselves, their motives and behaviors. One learns to take one's own inventory, to stop taking someone else's; this is a major shift in the projection and blaming that characterizes the addictive personality.

The first time a step is done with the class, it should be read (rotating readers by paragraph). The paragraphs are brief. Many of the students have difficulty reading and will act out rather than face embarrassment in the group. After the step has been read, each student is asked to comment on whatever aspect they choose in the step. They may agree or disagree with a certain sentence. They may offer a story that illustrates something described in the step when the step is done the second time with the class.

"The Steps To School Success: Student Workbook" contains the steps and worksheets for each step.

THE FIVE STEPS TO SCHOOL SUCCESS

STEP ONE:

"We admitted that we were failing in school, that the way we were thinking and living would not allow us to succeed."

It's hard to admit that the problem is one of our own making. It hurts to say: The way I've handled my schoolwork hasn't worked before, isn't working now and won't work tomorrow.

We can go on forever blaming others. Our parents don't help us enough. Our teachers don't give us enough chances. Classes are boring. Why do we need to know this anyway? We can keep saying and thinking those things and no one can make us stop. There's a certain feeling of power in that. But where is it really getting us?

Can we really feel good about ourselves when we aren't doing the things we know are expected of us? Can we feel okay when we're letting ourselves and the people who care about us down?

It feels humiliating to say: What I've been doing with my life isn't working. If I say that, will other people still care about me? Will anyone respect me at all? Isn't it better to keep on with my tough "I don't care and you can't make me" front? I might try to avoid the problem by saying: "I just haven't done my work because I didn't want to. But I'll do it now. Tomorrow I'll do my homework, I'll study for my test, I'll raise my hand in class and not goof around. I'll take notes. I'll do that tomorrow. I don't need to use a planner. I don't need to think about taking responsibility for failing in school. It makes me feel bad to think about this. That isn't good for me, is it? I'm not supposed to feel bad, am I?"

If I'm honest with myself, though, I know I do feel bad. I pretend it doesn't matter to me, but I feel bad about myself when I look at the kids who are doing well. They stand differently. They walk differently. Their voices sound different. It seems so hard sometimes that I'm afraid to try. If I try and fail, won't that be even worse? What if I really can't do the work?

We realized that all we had to do was take the first step. When we admitted that our way of doing our schoolwork wasn't working, then we have prepared the ground to plant something new.

STEP TWO:

*We made a commitment. We would follow, as exactly as we were able,
the program for school success that was being offered to us.*

For many students, this step seems almost impossible to imagine taking. First, we had made what felt like a shameful admission. We admitted that our own way of managing our schoolwork wasn't working and wouldn't work. Now we were told to approach our schoolwork, not as we saw fit, but according to someone else's plan. Inside we rebelled at this idea. We wanted to stand on our own two feet. We did not want to be babies following someone else's directions.

No one could make us learn. This was an absolute truth. Hadn't our parents and teachers been "on" us for years? Weren't people always trying to make us do our schoolwork?

We realized that the question was not about whether someone could control us. The question was: How were we going to use our own will?

We could use our will to try to do things our way (whether or not that was good for us). We could use our will to try to force other people to do things our way. These were approaches that all of us had already tried.

We could use our will for self-discipline. As best we were able, we could choose to walk the path that was being pointed out to us.

We took a leap of faith.

We made a commitment. We would follow, as exactly as we were able, the program for school success that was being offered to us. We let ourselves believe, that if we used our will correctly, if we made a full effort, we could and would succeed. WE SET THE GOAL. WE WANTED TO BE SUCCESSFUL IN HIGH SCHOOL. We would reach this goal by doing three things.

1. We would do all our homework every day.
We would come to school prepared.

Whenever possible, we would do our homework before we left school Otherwise, we would do our homework as soon as we got home. One day at a time, we would do our schoolwork before we did other things. Though we might not feel like we wanted to, or should need to, we would do our schoolwork first: before we earned money, watched television, spent time with girlfriends or boy-friends. In this way, we would be selfish. We would care about ourselves. We would act as if we believed and in time might come to believe ("fake it until you make it") that our schoolwork was our first responsibility.

We would do all our homework every night and study for our tests. We would come to school each day prepared.

2. We would arrive to class on time.

We would not allow ourselves to be lured into social situations and old habits. We would arrive at all our classes on time. Once there, we would listen and participate.

If we didn't understand what we were being taught, we would have the courage to ask a question. When necessary, we would ask for help. If someone thought we were "stupid," it would only be because they did not understand that we were trying.

3. We would treat our teachers with respect and our classmates with kindness.

We came to understand that we are all in this together. It was possible for all of us to succeed. It would happen if we all worked hard and helped each other. We would not like everyone. Even so, we would try not to add to the suffering that is already in the world.

We would follow the golden rule. We would "Do onto others as we would have others do onto us".

STEP THREE:

We understood and accepted the need for abstinence from alcohol and all other drugs.

For some of us, Step 3 was the hardest of all. It seemed that in order to succeed in school, we were being asked to give up everything that made us feel good. We didn't see anything the matter with needing a chemical to feel good. "Why can't we do both?" some of us asked. "What difference would it make if we had a few beers on the weekends?"

But that brought us right back to the first two Steps. Step 1: Our way of approaching school hadn't worked. Step 2: We had made a commitment to try the way that was being suggested to us here.

"Why no drugs, no drinking?" we asked. "Did they really have anything to do with our problems in school?"

Most of us had someone in our family who had an alcohol or drug problem. Certain behaviors and attitudes went along with that problem. Those of us who had mothers or fathers who were addicted had mostly promised ourselves that "it would never happen to us".

What if it already was happening to us? We knew something was wrong. What we were doing with our lives wasn't working. We were failing in school. People were angry and disappointed with us. It was really scary to admit this because we didn't know any other way to do things. We had put our energy into trying to convince our teachers and parents that "nothing" was wrong. When we failed, we said we didn't care.

Those of us who used chemicals, covered up and lied about it. When people confronted us with our chemical use, we got mad. We knew how to distract people from what was really going on. We were using alcohol and drugs.

It was easy to convince ourselves that there was no connection between the use of chemicals and the problems in our lives. Many of us really liked using chemicals. They made us feel good, high, not in pain.

Now we were being told that we would not be able to make the constant effort needed for school success if we continued to use. We would not be able to stay honest with ourselves and with others if we didn't stay straight. We'd grow up in our physical bodies. We'd gain adult rights. But if we kept on using now, we wouldn't really learn how to deal with people, how to be successful in our relationships and in our work.

What was at stake here was not a matter of having fun. What was at stake was our lives. We did want our lives to be better. We wanted to have some real control and choice about our futures. We agreed to do two things:

1. We would be straight and sober in school, every day.

2. We would listen and try to understand all the information that was presented to us about alcohol, drug use and addiction.

We would listen "soberly". We would let ourselves hear the information. We would not say "this is boring" or "we already know all this". From these first two steps we would decide whether we could take the third.

3. We would make an informed decision about whether we would abstain from alcohol and all other drugs in our lives.

If we decided to abstain and could not, we would ask for help.

Our teachers believed that every one of us could succeed. We would not be sitting in this room if they did not. We had been chosen to be here.

STEP FOUR:

We got honest with ourselves about the choices we made.

Most of us who were failing in school had a hard time feeling good about ourselves. We acted as if we didn't care. We said that only geeks did well in school. In our hearts, though, we did care. We knew we were messing up. We knew when we weren't living up to our responsibilities. For many of us, it had been this way since elementary school. By now we were afraid that even if we really tried, we could not succeed.

Many of us had been put down a lot. People had yelled at us, been critical of our efforts. When we felt bad, and bad about ourselves, some of us had used chemicals to get rid of those feelings. When we stopped using, it was hard to know what to do with our unhappiness.

Some of us felt angry. Some of us were angry with parents who had left us and disappointed us. We were angry at teachers who hadn't helped us succeed. Most of us had a lot of resentments. It seemed to make us feel better to have someone else to blame. It can be easier to be angry with someone else then to be honest about how we feel about ourselves.

A lot of us don't think much of ourselves. We might act like we didn't think much of anyone else. We could take someone else's inventory - and be pretty harsh about it too. But what about how we felt about our own actions? Some of us started to get honest with ourselves. We stopped listening to our ownexcuses. Some of us learned to stop ourselves from arguing back when we knew we were wrong. Some of us started to expect more of ourselves.

We stopped settling for sloppy half-done homework. We spent that extra hour studying for a test.
We stopped pretending that it was no big deal if we "forgot" our books, our planners.
We stopped acting like it was okay not to bring a pencil to school.
We stopped looking for someone else to blame. We started facing the truth.

Just because we wished that something wasn't true wasn't a good enough reason not to deal with truth. We stopped using our energy to pretend and fool ourselves. When we faced the truth, we discovered we could cope with it better than we'd thought.

When we were tempted to argue, or lie, when we were told things we didn't want to hear, we learned to slow ourselves down. We started trying TO DO THE RIGHT THINGS.
We stopped trying to "get away" with stuff. We stopped avoiding things.
We stopped asking ourselves, "How can I get out of this?" when we were confronted with a problem.

We learned to ask ourselves, "What is the right thing to do here?""Is there someone who will help me do the right thing?"

Our lives got better. When we were honest with ourselves, we liked ourselves better. When we liked ourselves better, we were nicer to other people. They, in turn, were nicer to us.
We got honest with ourselves. We got stronger. Our lives got better.

STEP FIVE:

We would bring something of ourselves, beyond our schoolwork, to school.
We began to contribute our talents and energy in a way that seemed right for us.

Being successful in school turned out to be about more than completion of our work. Real success in school also included INVOLVEMENT.

In Step Five, we began to think about our connection to our school. Most of us couldn't wait to get out the door. We wanted "out of here", to hang out with our friends, or in front of the television, or to play video games.

Why in the world would we want to stay around? Wasn't that for "dweebs"? Who did these after school things anyway? Community service, school plays, sports, art exhibits? Those things weren't for us.

When we stayed honest with ourselves, which we were trying hard to do, we knew there was more to the story. We didn't stay around partly because we had "better" things to do, but also partly because we didn't know where we'd fit in.

We felt like outsiders. Most of us didn't have a lot of confidence. What if we couldn't find friends? What if we didn't fit in with those kids? Instead we did what we had learned to do so well! We avoided the situations that made us uncomfortable. We acted like we were too cool for that stuff, like we didn't care.

Some of us had really bad memories about after-school activities. We remembered being the last kid picked for team sports. We remembered being laughed at for things we tried to do. Some of us never had the right clothes to fit in. Maybe there wasn't money to pay for these things or someone to drive us.

Now Step Five told us that to be successful in school, we needed greater involvement. How would we know what to do? Where would we fit? We were told to think about what we liked to do, what had we enjoyed doing when we were little kids.

What was fun?

Some of us didn't think we had any talent. Our teachers told us that wasn't possible. Everyone had something to contribute to the world. Right now, our world was school.

We only had to follow our hearts.

Did we like to run? We could try out for track. If we'd played soccer and enjoyed it, maybe we would play again. If we liked to draw, then we might join the art club. We could get involved in the next student play. If we didn't like to draw or act or sing, maybe we would join the yearbook staff.

We might follow our interest to find our talents. We might do something that mattered to us for other reasons. If we knew someone who had been injured or died in an alcohol-related car accident, we might decide to join SADD.

We would bring something of ourselves to school beyond our classwork. We would get involved. We would do something at school that we liked to do. Maybe we'd find out that we could really be part of things, "a part" instead of "apart". Who knows? Maybe we'd get to like school!

D. Outcome

Despite the by now expected complaints, the meetings went well. The students read, which all of them needed to do, and the structure helped them stay on track.

They tolerated the meetings because we paired them with hot chocolate. If recovering alcoholics drank coffee at their meetings, we reasoned that recovering school failures should drink hot chocolate at theirs.

The program turned. Maybe the steps were the significant factor. More likely, it was simply the end of the semester, time to come around or exercise their right to leave.

Every "LifeSkills" student had signed up for another elective second semester. They were transferring to Sewing, Study Hall, or our personal favorite, "Foods of the World" (a perfect unconscious selection given their intense hunger and what AA calls "fantasies of a geographic cure".)

With or without the original students, we were going ahead with the pilot. We met with a group of about twenty other freshmen and introduced the program. We told them that "LifeSkills" was a small class for students doing poorly in school who wanted to do better.

"Was it true that we took trips sometimes?" they wanted to know. "Would we still be having snacks?" We told them that yes, those things would continue. We invited students to apply for acceptance. An encouraging number requested an interview.

We reminded the original students that the class would be larger the second semester. Though other students had applied, any of the original students who wished to continue in "LifeSkills" (and were committed to getting down to "productivity") would be given priority. Students who did not stay in "LifeSkills" were welcome to continue meeting with the intern for individual counseling.

The boys who had been in treatment with Barbara approached her ten days before finals. They wanted to stay in "LifeSkills"; they were desperate to stay. They had not been ready for the help we were offering them. They insisted that they were now. They had friends who wanted to enroll. They would help us with the new students. Perhaps they could co-teach with us?

In conjunction with the guidance counselor, who would need to authorize their withdrawal from "Foods of the World," we took a hard line with them: they would need to demonstrate over the remaining ten days that they could deliver on their promises.

The power base had shifted.

There is a moment when a stepparent knows that she has forged a relationship with someone else's child. Only then may (s)he impose discipline without the child becoming resentful. Barbara and I had earned the right to make some demands. Probably we had earned it awhile before, but now it was acknowledged.

Once the boys "went public" with their decision, the girls followed. At the end of the first semester, all six "LifeSkills" students had re-enrolled. The girl who had been the most disdainful asked whether we could keep her change of heart a secret from her mother. Then students from another freshmen team came to complain. "The students on your team get all the good things. They get LifeSkills."

We *knew* we had established ourselves.Our students, who needed us so much and had battled us so fiercely, were becoming "teachable". We were over-subscribed with new students and had to turn several away. We started the second semester having increased our enrollment as much as we dared. We took twelve.

VII. How to Teach "LifeSkills":
Policies and Suggested Materials

It is on the subject of curriculum that the divergence in orientation between teachers and counselors/ clinicians come to the forefront. The central thrust of traditional social work education has always been on the growth of the self in the context of a helping relationship, that is, on relatedness. The starting point for clinicians is with process, not content. Teachers' training generally emphasizes method and curriculum. Nonetheless, every teacher knows that what works with one class may fail with another.

What needs to be stated at once in that the essentials of the "Counselors in the Classroom" design lie more so in its structure than in its content. The sine qua non for high-risk students is the establishment of a relationship of sufficient value (*i.e.*, cathexis) and longevity that the youth become, with that adult, in that setting, "teachable".

There is no magic curriculum, no worksheet, no software, print-out or video that can be handed over. It is a question, rather, of creating an educational structure in which relatedness may develop. What is essential to the model, what I consider the hardware of the system, is that:

(1)   Students are seen, initially daily, for credit, in a small group class (maximum of 12).

(2)   A behavior modification system that reinforces behaviors appropriate to school and life success is utilized. The rewards in the system are earned for the group as a whole, that is, "my good effort benefits all of us".

(3)   Staff undertake the class expecting that they are beginning relationships that will continue through the duration of the students' enrollment in that school. The design and frequency of the contact will likely evolve, but the goal is to bond students to faculty, school and peers.

(4)   Group process, the social learning and identification that occurs in the group, is more significant than specific content.

Clare LaMeres says it eloquently: "The content is simply the vehicle that we use to teach kids about life."

There is no shortage of curriculum materials (*i.e.*, software). Suggestions for specific content areas and existing materials will follow. More important is that the particular counselor and teacher feel able to combine their own expertise and specialization with the essentials of the model.

The design could be integrated into a health class, could be lead by a librarian working in tandem with a counselor or by an art teacher. The health teacher's sequence might be in "Relationships", "Addictions", "Mental Health", and "Family Life".

An English teacher or librarian might design a curriculum that focused on literature in which adversity is overcome, despair and depression turned into creativity, and issues of integrity play a central role.

A Title One teacher might choose to focus her class on study skills, utilizing the essentials (i.e., small-group, long-term relationships, plus behavior modification to reinforce the group for socially appropriate behaviors). A physical education teacher could work with a counselor using a Project Adventure approach to team building. A social studies teacher could look at a "History of Family Life". An art teacher might integrate art-therapy methods and themes into curriculum. A counselor could work with ALP students two to three periods weekly.

This said, there are some Do's and Don'ts and some biases about content areas that we believe are useful in incorporate. These follow.

A. Dos and Don'ts for Classroom Management

Dos:

Do select students based on faculty recommendations, if possible during the spring. Optimally this course should be initiated first semester of the first year at the middle or high school level.

Do talk with parents and recommended students before they are enrolled. If it is possible to meet individually, do so. If not, hold preliminary meetings with small groups of referred students. At the very least, make contact directly with the student by telephone.

Do team teach whenever possible. The ideal teaching team for LifeSkills is made up of a teacher and a counselor. Try to be in the classroom together once weekly, if possible. The students benefit when they see adults working together as a cohesive team..

Do be sure you have a basic compatibility and respect for your colleague. You will need to support each other..

Do seat the students in a circle.

Do set limits.

Do use behavior modification. There are abundant options. Reinforce punctuality, good grades, participation, respect and cooperation. Let the group selects the goals. Trips are popular and further the goal of bonding the group. We learned how to drive a van.

Do use our student workbook "The Steps To School Success". The workbook contains the steps and accompanying work sheets and the central organizational tool these students require, the planner. Students are expected to have their workbooks with them every day.

Do begin each class by asking to see each student's workbook. Credit in the behavioral system is earned when the student has the planner and has written assignments for the day in the planner. Allow students to scurry around trying to write down assignments they have missed. Don't penalize them. What matters is that they are trying to get the assignment.

Do use primary reinforcers OFTEN, such as hot chocolate, popcorn, juice, COOKIES.

Do notice and comment on gains, no matter how small. Look hard for the positives.

Do use Clare LaMeres' technique. When a student enters the classroom, make eye contact and shake his or her hand.[1]

Do establish group rules right away. Convey a "nobody gets left out, all of us can succeed if we work together" motto.

Do Remember that the lives of these students are often full of sadness and crises. Do allow them to utilize class time to process their feelings and help them support one another.

Don'ts

Don't accept students who don't want to enroll. Once enrolled, **don't** let students drop the course without a parent conference.

Don't get caught in power struggles. When a student is pushing the limits, talk to him from nearby and talk softly. Try to offer a face-saving exit.

Don't expect steady progress. You aren't going to cure most high-risk students. It will be a lot if you can travel with them. If you don't, chances are no one else will.

Don't think this is going to be easy.

Don't let one student put down another. Don't let them "take each others' inventories."

Don't neglect to maintain contact with parents.

Don't be put off by disrespectful manners. Notice whether students are doing what you ask them to. Adolescents show their respect by acceding to our rules, not by their demeanor when they do so.

Don't let students "split" you and other faculty. Consider inviting the faculty person about whom they are complaining to come to class and talk things out.

Don't overlook symptoms of drug abuse. (See appendix)

Don't be afraid to have guest speakers. All visitors are potential guest speakers. Engage the students in "interviewing" them.

Don't forget the COOKIES.

B. Recommended Content of Curriculum

The Massachusetts Common Core of Learning, as excerpted on page 11 of this manuscript, points us right to the curriculum.

We began "LifeSkills" by prioritizing goal setting. This decision was grounded in the work of Gordon Allport: "The possession of long-range goals, regarded as central to one's personal existence, distinguishes the human being from the animal, the adult from the child, and in many cases, the healthy personality from the sick".

"The intentional nature of the healthy personality - this striving toward the future - unifies and integrates the total personality. However beset by problems and conflicts a person may be...the personality can, in a sense, be made whole by integrating all its aspects toward the achieving of goals and intentions"[1].

Clearly related to goal setting were productivity, organization and planning. From there, we intended to emphasize:

      1) Critical-thinking skills
      2) Decision making
      3) A focus on reality versus denial and avoidance

What we discovered astounded us. Almost without exception, OUR STUDENTS DID NOT KNOW THE GOLDEN RULE. What it may be necessary to conclude from that one piece of information was the subject of the April 30, 1995 New York Times Magazine cover story: "Who'll Teach Kids Right From Wrong?" (Roger Rosenblatt). The article describes the work of Thomas Lickona, a developmental psychologist and a professor of education at the State University of New York, a leader in the burgeoning character-education movement.

Before we could get to the Core of Learning goals, we would need to begin with the basic qualities of honesty and decency, fairness, and hard work - "The virtue", Likona says "of striving toward virtue"[2]. Traditionally, such teachings have not fallen under the auspices of the school (*i.e.*, the state) but to the family and church. The breakdown in the American family and the concomitant departure from ongoing religious education has left a chasm. That chasm is a national crisis.

The school has no choice but to respond. To do so effectively calls for conditions that can be provided by the presence of counselors in the classroom. What we greatted as appalling news ("They don't know the Golden Rule??!!?") only confirmed our conviction about the importance of the job we were trying to do.

CURRICULUM RESOURCES FOR AT-RISK GROUPS

Materials from any of the following may be adapted for groups of At-Risk middle or high school students. There are many other resources to be found in the various catalogues that come across all of our desks. Most counselors and teachers have already worked with similar curriculum components, and will want to incorporate their own materials.

Bea, R. (1992). The Four Conditions of Self-Esteem (Second Edition). Santa Cruz, CA: ETR Associates.

Dossick, J. & Shea, E. (1990) Creative Therapy I & Creative Therapy II: Exercises for Groups & 52 More Exercises for Groups. Sarasota, FL: Professional Resource Exchange, Inc.

Fetro, J.V. (1992). Personal and Social Skills: Understanding and Integrating Competencies Across Health Content. Santa Cruz, CA: ETR Associates.

Freeman, S.M. (1989). From Peer Pressure to Peer Support: Alcohol/Drug Prevention Through Group Process. Minneapolis, MN: Johnson Institute.

Kramer, Patricia. The Dynamics of Relationships. A Guide for Developing Self-Esteem and Social Skills for Teens and Young Adults.

Lions,   Quest: Skills for Adolescence. Quest International/Revised & Expanded. 1995.

LeMeres, C. (1994). Strengthening the Achievement, Motivation and Responsibility of AT-RISK Students: Resource Handbook. Bellevue, WA: Bureau of Education and Research.

Muldoon, J.A. (1988). Insight Class Program (with facilitator's guide and student workbook, My Life). Minneapolis, MN: Community Intervention, Inc.

O'Connor, B. (1994). A Guide for Teens: does Your Friend Have an Alcohol or Other Drug Problem? What Can You Do To Help? Cambridge, MA: Harvard School of Public Health.

Schmitz, Connie. Fighting Invisible Tigers: a 12-Part Course in Life Skills Development. Teachers Guide. Free Spirit Publishing (1987)

Simon, S., Howe, L. & Kirschenbaum, H. Values Clarification: A Handbook of Practical Strategies for Teachers and Students. New York: Hart Publishing Co., Inc.

The Study Skills Group (1986). Study Skills Program (Revised Edition edited by David Marshak. Reston, VA: The National Association of Secondary School Principals.

Wechsler, Beth (1995). The Steps To School Success. Falmouth, MA. Gosnold.

VIII. Selling the Program to Administration

Dennis Yarmouth Regional High School, the pilot site for the model, differed from many high schools in the openness of the principal, Curtis Collins, to experimentation. His advice for "selling" the model to other principals is that the counselor or teacher interested in implementing the program "needs to do his homework".

How can the program be fit into the schedule? How will staffing be coordinated? What role will the counselor play? These, Collins advises, are the counselor's homework.

1. Be prepared to present the model's central aspects.

2. The Massachusetts "Buzz Words" are the connection to:
    *Meeting TIME IN LEARNING REQUIREMENTS
    *DIRECT SUPPORT OF TEACHING AND LEARNING
    *RESTRUCTURING counseling services.

3. Address issues related to elective credits, school committee approval if needed, parent consent.

4. "Counselors in the Classroom" means you are teaching a course. It has to be scheduled as a course. It cannot replace administrative duties.

5. Recruit at least one other colleague to team teach. Think about additional staffing. Will the police work with you? The nurse? The assistant principal? Can you get an intern?

6. Based on your building and the teaching team, decide where in the curriculum the model fits. Is it a course for entering freshmen (our model)? Returning dropouts? Students with frequent suspensions?

7. Think longitudinally. Plan an approach that will keep the same counselors and faculty connected to the target population throughout their time in your building.

8. Seek referrals from faculty and go directly to the students. Tell them straight out: This is a course for students who are doing poorly in school and who want to do better.

9. Meet, either individually or in groups of two or three, with students who express an interest in the course. Assess whether the student is motivated and whether his life experience is congruent with the high-risk population the course targets. Most of our students are children of substance abusers. Most are not living in intact family systems. Many admit to past alcohol or drug use. (No one is ever still using when we meet them.)

10. If you are not already familiar with the Anonymous programs, go to some step meetings.

11. Call Gosnold (508-540-6550) to purchase the student workbooks "The Steps To School ` Success" and to arrange for technical assistance. We will design a package that fits your building needs and your budget.*

12. Talk to the grant writers in your system. "Counselors in the Classroom" is a highly flexible model. More importantly, the targeted population is like the proverbial elephant - you can grab hold of it from different ends.

* *Order form on last page.*

Questions and Answers

Q: *Can schools implement this model ourselves or do we require an outside clinician?*

A: Some of the research suggests that involvement of an agency outside the school has advantages. We believe the model can be implemented "either way".

Many schools already have clinicians from outside agencies delivering services on site. These clinicians are often available for additional hours (and will usually be willing to participate in grantwriting to fund their hours), or may be open to restructuring their existing role.

Guidance counselors and school adjustment counselors, working as a team with a teacher, can also implement "Counselors in the Classroom" model. They will require administrative support to reduce less essential duties.

Q.   *Does Gosnold provide consultation? What expenses are involved?*

A: Telephone consultation is available at no charge by calling Beth Wechsler at 508-540-6550.

Full day trainings are offered at Gosnold in the fall and spring. Rates are moderate, CEUs are available.

We will also come to you. Where school budgets allow, we recommend a full day staff training to introduce the model to all interested personnel, followed by two or three follow-up consultations, once the program is underway, for those faculty who go on to implement the model. In most instances this package includes materials which costs less than $2,000.

We will provide the necessary information to assist you in incorporating any of these options into grant proposals.

Q.   *What do we need "in house" to do this?*

A.   A minimum of one professional (counselor or teacher, both is ideal) who want to bring "Counselors in the Classroom" to their school, and an administrator who understands the needs of high risk youth. A budget of less than $500. funds the student workbook, "The Steps to School Success", reinforcers (including trips) and a full day training at Gosnold.

Q.   *How important is it to do this?*

A.   "Kids are dying every day...They're just dying more slowly"[1].

 **IX. Status Report**

January, 1998

    "Counselors in the Classroom" originated at Dennis Yarmouth Regional High School in September, 1994. Of the eleven students who participated in the pilot, nine remain in local schools.

    All of the students at DYRHS have maintained contact with Barbara Crellin and with each other. The girls have met weekly in group counselling since their sophomore year.

    Of the nine students, one transferred to the vocational school where we are told she has done very well. One student left school in response to chronic and life-threatening illness in her younger sibling. She has since completed a GED and intends to go on to the community college.

    Of the remaining seven students, two have been on honor roll and one of these recently received an invitation to apply to the United States Air Force Academy. One is a cheerleader and on graduation this spring hopes to become a flight attendant. Another student has maintained good grades and will attend the community college next year. One student transferred to private school where he was slowed down a grade. One has remained in school but done poorly. Two dropped out in the fall of their senior year but expect to return this semester.

    All of the students have contended with ongoing hardships and upheaval in their personal lives throughout the years that we have known them.

    Funding from the Massachusetts Governor's Alliance Against Drugs enabled us to transition the model to Falmouth's grade 7-8 Lawrence School in March, 1996. The junior high school course is housed within the reading program. Lucille Flynn, English and Social Studies department chair, has brought thirty years of teaching experience to the pilot. Reading is an ideal subject area, allowing the course to function as a bibliotherapy group.

    At the high school level, Barbara Crellin has been anxious to try a gender specific approach. She taught a girls-only LifeSkills section (again at DYRHS) in 1997. Working with English teacher Mary Ellen Strote and counseling intern Ann Temple, seven high risk girls met three times weekly. The girls had been identified by administration and faculty for a combination of disciplinary problems and school failure. Most were using drugs. They made dramatic reversals within two months.

    During the 1996-97 school year, a second $8,000 grant from the Massachusetts Governor's Alliance Against Drugs, brought the CIC model to Martha's Vineyard Regional High School. School Adjustment Counselor Beverly Mann sent a memo to staff about the program. Special Education teacher Juanita Espino stepped up to team with her, bringing the model into the special needs arena (where it readily fits) for the first time. Again, the results were strong. A class of students, all ineligible for school sports due to their grades, made sufficient gains to all be sports eligible within two months.

    These additional sections have confirmed what we learned in our first pilot. Students need to "elect" the course. It appears that we make better progress when we allow students the first semester of their freshman year without intervention. Being "proactive" on their behalf may mean we intervene too far above the proverbial "bottom."

    June, 1997 NIDA Notes brought us news of "Reconnecting Youth" (RY). Underway in the Seattle Public Schools, RY also utilizes as its core a one semester personal growth class for high risk adolescents and shares the fundamental goals of bonding/reconnecting high risk youth to faculty and peers and reducing alcohol and drug use. A field tested curriculum is available for RY. NIDA, which has funded the project, reports encouraging data.

    Also encouraging, a September 10, 1997 editorial in the *Journal of the American Medical Association* reported the first research findings from the National Longitudinal Study on Adolescent Health (the ADD Health Study). Adolescents who are well connected to school were consistently found to engage in less risky activities than those less well connected to schools.

    Gosnold efforts to obtain significant funding for the CIC project have not been successul to date. As with many social service programs for children, even small amounts of funding needed for each site have been difficult to obtain.

    CIC has been presented throughout New England. At conferences held by the Massachusetts School Counselors Association, National Association of Social Workers, Harvard Graduate School of Education, the National Conference on the Adolescent, and the Cape Cod Symposium on Addictions, we have been met by our colleagues with interest and enthusiasm.

    A school needs a counselor, a teacher, and an administrator interested in the model to bring it to their building. If we can be of any assistance, please call us at (508) 563-9202.

Regards,
Beth Wechsler, M.S.W.

All of our grant proposals include stipends for teachers and counselors, and a budget for materials and reinforcers as well as ongoing consultation. We would be glad to include your school or non-profit agency. So please, keep us posted!

Bibliography/References

"The Twelve Steps and Twelve Traditions." (1982). Alcoholics Anonymous World Services, Inc. 23rd Printing

American Medical Association (1990). America's Adolescents: How Healthy Are They?

Bea, R (1992). The Four Conditions of Self-esteem (Second Edition) Santa Cruz, CA: ETR Associates.

Carnegie Council on Adolescent Development (1989). Turning Points: Preparing American Youth for the 21st Century.

Dossick, J. & Shea, E. (1990). Creative Therapy I & Creative Therapy II: Exercises for Groups & 52 More Exercises for Groups. Sarasota, FL: Professional Resource Exchange, Inc.

Dryfoos, J. (1994). Full Service Schools: A Revolution in Health and Social Services for Children, Youth, and Families, Jossey-Bass.

Eagle, Jeff (February 11, 1996). Stoned In The Hall: Our Kids on Drugs, Sean Polay, Sunday Cape Cod Times, Hyannis, MA

Fetro, J.V. (1992). Personal and Social Skills: Understanding and Integrating Competencies Across Health Content. Santa Cruz, CA: ETR Associates

Freeman, S.M. (1989). From Peer Pressure to Peer Support: Alcohol/Drug Prevention through Group Process. Minneapolis, MN: Johnson Institute.

Hewlett, S. (1992) When the Bough Breaks: The Cost of Neglecting Our Children. Harper Collins.

Kramer, Patricia. The Dynamics of Relationships. A Guide for Developing Self-Esteem and Social Skill for Teens and Young Adults.

LeMeres, Clare (1994). Strengthening the Achievement, Motivation and Responsiibility of AT-RISK Students: Resource Handbook. Bellevue, WA: Bureau of Education and Research.

Lions-Quest (1995). Quest: skills for Adolescence. Quest International/Revised & Expanded.

Massachusetts Department of Education (1994). A Focus on Attention Deficits.

Muldoon, J.A. (1988). Insight Class Program (With facilitator's guide and student workbook, My Life.) Minneapolis, MN: Community Intervention, Inc.

Nakken, Craig (1991) The Addictive Personality. Hazelton.

National Commission on the Role of the School and the Community in Improving Adolescent Health (1990). Code Blue: Uniting for Healthier Youth. NASBE, Alexandria, VA.

National Forum on the Future of Children and Families: (1989). Social Policy for Children and Families: Creating an Agenda. National Forum on the Future of Children and Families, Washington, D.C.

National Health/Education Consortium. (1990). Crossing the Boundaries Between Health and Education. National Commission to Prevent Infant Mortality, Washington, D.C.

O'Connor, B. (1994). a Guide for Teens: Does Your Friend Have an Alcohol or Other Drug Problem? What Can You do To Help? Harvard School of Public Health, Cambridge, MA.

Oursler, Fulton and Will (1949). Father Flannagan of Boys Town. Doubleday & Co., Garden City, NY

Roos, Stephen. A Yound Person's Guide to the 12 Steps.

Rosenblatt, Roger (April 30, 1995). Who'll Teach Kids Right From Wrong? New York Times Magazine, New York, NY.

Schorr, Lisbeth B. and Daniel (1987). Within Our Reach: Breaking the Cycle of Disadvantage. Anchor Book.

Schmitz, connie. (1987). Fighting Invisible Tigers: A 12-Part Course in Life Skills Development. Teachers Guide. Free Spirit Publishing.

Simon, S., Howe, L. & Kirschenbaum, H. Values Clarification: A Handbook of Practical Strategies for Teachers and Students. Hart Publishing Co., Inc. New York, NY.

The Study Skills Group (1986). Study Skills Program (Revised Edition, edited by David Marshak). The National Association of Secondary School Prinicipals, Reston, VA.

PREFACE

   1. **Code Blue: Uniting for a Healthier Youth**. 1990. National Commission on the Role of School and Community in Improving Adolescent Health, Executive Summary. NASBE.

   2. **Adolescents at Risk: Prevalence and Prevention**. Joy G. Dryfoos. 1990. Oxford University Press.

CHAPTER III

   1. **Creating an Agenda for School-Based Health: A Review of Selected Reports.** Harvard School Health Education Project, Department of Health and Social Behavior, Harvard School of Public Health.

   2. **Social Policy for Children and Families: Creating an Agenda.** National Forum on the Future of Children and Families, Institute of Medicine, National Research Council, National Academy of Sciences. 1989.

   3. **Code Blue: Uniting for Healthier Youth.**

   4. **America's Adolescents: How Healthy Are They?** American Medical Association (AMA). 1990.

   5. **Adolescents at Risk: Prevalence and Prevention.** Joy G. Dryfoos.

   6. **Turning Points: Preparing American Youth for the 21st Century.** Carnegie Council on Adolescent Development, Task Force on Education of Young Adolescents. 1989.

   7. **When the Bough Breaks: The Cost of Neglecting Our Children.** Sylvia A. Hewlett, Harper Collins, 1992.

   8. **Code Blue: Uniting for a Healthier You.**

   9. **Creating and Agenda for School-Based Health Promotion: A Review of Selected Reports.**

   10. **Adolescents as Risk: Prevalence and Prevention.** Joy G. Dryfoos.

   11. **Within our Reach: Breaking the Cycle of Disadvantage.** Lisbeth B. Schorr and Daniel Schorr. 1987. Anchor Book.

   12. *IBID*

   13. **Adolescents at Risk: Prevalence and Prevention.** Joy G. Dryfoos.

CHAPTER IV

   1. **Skills for Adolescents — Revised and Expanded.** Lions-Quest. 1995.

CHAPTER V

   1. **A Focus on Attention Deficits.** Massachusetts Department of Education. 1994.

CHAPTER VI

   1. **The Addictive Personality.** Craig Nakken.

   2. **The Twelve Steps and Twelve Traditions.** Alcoholics Anonymous World Services, Inc. 23rd printing, 1982.

CHAPTER VII

   1. **Strengthening the Achievement, Motivation, and Responsibility of At-Risk Students: Resource Handbook.** Clare LeMeres. Bureau of Education and Research, 1994.

   2. **Who'll Teach Kids Right From Wrong?** Roger Rosenblatt. <u>New York Times Magazine</u>, April 30, 1995.

   3. **Father Flannagan of Boys Town.**

QUESTIONS AND ANSWERS

   1. Jeff Eagle, Ph. D., Cape Psych Center, **Stoned in the Halls: Our Kids on Drugs,** Sean Polay, <u>Sunday Cape Cod Times</u>, February 11, 1996.

Materials Order Form

"Counselors in the Classroom"
for Mainstream Intervention With High Risk Youth

☐ Sample Copy: "The Steps to School Success" (student workbook) —*$10.00*

☐ Set (10) Student Workbooks ("The Steps to School Success")
 with (1) Counselor-Teacher Guide — *$95.00*

Sub-total:$_____

Shipping: *$3.00*

Total: $_____

Name: _____

Position: _____

School/Agency Name: _____

Address: _____

_____

Mail with check payable to **Beth Wechsler**
Counselors in the Classroom
P.O. Box 1721
No. Falmouth, MA 02556